THE CHILDREN'S BOOK OF CAROLS

Also available from Blackie

The Children's Book of Prayers

THE CHILDREN'S BOOK OF CAROLS

Arranged by John Brush
Illustrated by Shirley Tourret

BLACKIE

ACKNOWLEDGEMENTS

The publishers would like to thank the following for their kind permission to reproduce copyright material in this book:

A.P. Watt Ltd on behalf of the Estate of Frances Chesterton for the words of 'How Far is it to Bethlehem?'; Oxford University Press for the text of 'Zither Carol' by Malcolm Sargent and the melody of 'Rocking' collected by M. Shaw.

These arrangements Copyright © 1988 John Brush
Illustrations © 1988 Shirley Tourret
First published 1988 by Blackie & Son Ltd

All rights reserved. No part of this publication may be reproduced, stored in a retrieval system, or transmitted in any form or by any means, electronic, mechanical, photocopying, recording or otherwise without the written permission of the Publishers.

British Library Cataloguing in Publication Data
The Children's book of carols.
1. Carols, English
I. Tourret, Shirley
783.6'32 0942   M1738

ISBN 0 216 92339 5

Blackie and Son Ltd
7 Leicester Place
London WC2H 7BP

Music Origination by
Barnes Music Engraving Ltd
East Sussex TN22 4HA
Printed in Great Britain by Scotprint Ltd., Musselburgh

Contents

Gabriel's Message	12
Away in a Manger	14
Infant Holy	16
Rocking	17
Once in Royal David's City	18
O Little Town of Bethlehem	20
O Come All Ye Faithful	22
Hark! The Herald Angels Sing	24
How Far is it to Bethlehem?	26
Zither Carol	28
Silent Night	30
Good Christian Men, Rejoice	32
I Saw Three Ships	33
Il Est Né Le Divin Enfant	34
Unto us a Child is Born	36
God Rest You Merry Gentlemen	38
Sans Day Carol	40
The Holly and the Ivy	42
In the Bleak Mid-Winter	44
Masters in this Hall	46
Patapan	48
Tomorrow Shall Be My Dancing Day	49
Up! Good Christen Folk and Listen	50
Good King Wenceslas	52
Shepherds! Shake off Your Drowsy Sleep	54
The First Nowell	56

We Wish You a Merry Christmas	**58**
Here We Come A-Wassailing	**60**
We Three Kings	**62**
O'er the Hill and o'er the Vale	**64**
Easter Eggs	**65**
Coventry Carol	**66**
The Twelve Days of Christmas	**68**
The Infant King	**70**
The Birds	**72**
This Joyful Eastertide	**74**
Index of First Lines	**77**

THE CHILDREN'S BOOK OF
CAROLS

Gabriel's Message

2. 'For known a blessed Mother thou shalt be,
   All generations laud and honour thee,
   Thy son shall be Emmanuel, by seers foretold.
     Most highly favour'd lady.'
     Gloria

3. Then gentle Mary meekly bowed her head,
   'To me be as it pleaseth God,' she said,
   'My soul shall laud and magnify his holy name.'
     Most highly favour'd lady.
     Gloria

4. Of her, Emmanuel, the Christ, was born
   In Bethlehem, all on a Christmas morn,
   And Christian folk throughout the world will ever say—
     Most highly favour'd lady.
     Gloria

Away in a Manger

2. The cattle are lowing, the baby awakes;
   But little Lord Jesus, no crying he makes:
   I love thee Lord Jesus; look down from the sky,
   And stay by my side until morning is nigh.

3. Be near me Lord Jesus; I ask thee to stay
   Close by me for ever, and love me, I pray;
   Bless all the dear children in thy tender care,
   And fit us for heaven to live with thee there.

Infant Holy

**The angel Gabriel from heaven came
His wings as drifted snow**

*O come, all ye faithful
Joyful and triumphant*

*How silently, how silently
The wondrous gift is given*

We will rock you
We will serve you all we can

Rocking

Once in Royal David's City

2. He came down to earth from heaven
   Who is God and Lord of all,
   And his shelter was a stable,
   And his cradle was a stall;
   With the poor and mean and lowly
   Lived on earth our Saviour holy.

3. And through all his wondrous childhood
   He would honour and obey,
   Love and watch the lowly maiden,
   In whose gentle arms he lay:
   Christian children all must be,
   Mild, obedient, good as he.

4. For he is our childhood's pattern,
   Day by day like us he grew,
   He was little, weak, and helpless,
   Tears and smiles like us he knew:
   And he feeleth for our sadness,
   And he shareth in our gladness.

5. And our eyes at last shall see him,
   Through his own redeeming love,
   For that child so dear and gentle
   Is our Lord in heaven above;
   And he leads his children on
   To the place where he is gone.

6. Not in that poor lowly stable,
   With the oxen standing by,
   We shall see him; but in heaven,
   Set at God's right hand on high;
   Where like stars his children crowned
   All in white shall wait around.

O Little Town of Bethlehem

2. O morning stars, together
   Proclaim thy holy birth.
   And praises sing to God the King
   And peace to men on earth.
   For Christ is born of Mary
   And, gathered all above
   While mortals sleep, the angels keep
   Their watch of wondering love.

3. How silently, how silently,
   The wondrous gift is given!
   So God imparts to human hearts
   The blessings of his heaven.
   No ear may hear his coming;
   But in this world of sin,
   Where meek souls will receive him, still
   The dear Christ enters in.

4. O holy child of Bethlehem,
   Descend to us we pray;
   Cast out our sin, and enter in,
   Be born in us today.
   We hear the Christmas angels
   The great glad tidings tell:
   O come to us, abide with us,
   Our Lord Emmanuel.

O Come all Ye Faithful

2. God of God
   Light of Light,
   Lo! He abhors not the Virgin's womb;
   Very God,
   Begotten, not created:

   O come let us adore him
   O come let us adore him,
   O come let us adore him,
   Christ the Lord.

3. Sing, choirs of angels,
   Sing in exultation,
   Sing, all you citizens of heaven above;
   Glory to God
   In the highest:

   O come let us etc.

4. Yea, Lord, we greet thee,
   Born this happy morning,
   Jesu, to thee be glory given;
   Word of the father,
   Now in flesh appearing:

   O come let us etc.

Hark! The Herald Angels Sing

Hark! The her-ald an-gels sing, 'Glo - ry — to the new-born King'.

2. Christ, by highest heaven adored,
Christ, the everlasting Lord,
Late in time behold him come,
Offspring of a virgin's womb.
Veiled in flesh the Godhead see;
Hail, the Incarnate Deity,
Pleased as Man with man to dwell,
Jesus, our Emmanuel!

*Hark! The herald angels sing,
'Glory to the new-born King'.*

3. Hail, the heaven-born Prince of Peace!
Hail, the Sun of Righteousness!
Light and life to all he brings,
Risen with healing in his wings.
Mild he lays his glory by,
Born that man no more may die,
Born to raise the sons of earth,
Born to give them second birth.

*Hark! The herald angels sing,
'Glory to the new-born King'.*

How Far is it to Bethlehem?

3. May we stroke the creatures there
   Ox, ass or sheep?
   May we peep like them and see
   Jesus asleep?

4. If we touch his tiny hand
   Will he awake?
   Will he know we've come so far
   Just for his sake?

5. Great kings have precious gifts,
   And we have naught.
   Little smiles and little tears are
   All we brought.

6. For all weary children
   Mary must weep,
   Here on his bed of straw,
   Sleep, children, sleep.

7. God's in his mother's arms;
   Babes in the byre,
   Sleep as they sleep who find
   Their heart's desire.

Zither Carol

2. Shepherds came – at the fame – of thy name,
   Angels their guide to Bethlehem.
   In that place – saw thy face – filled with grace,
   Stood at thy door.

   'Hallelujah' the church bells ring,
   'Hallelujah' the angels sing
   'Hallelujah' from ev'rything.
   Love evermore.

3. Wise men too – hast to do – homage new,
   Gold, myrrh and frankincense they bring.
   As 'twas said – starlight led to thy bed,
   Bending their knee.

   'Hallelujah' the church bells ring,
   'Hallelujah' the angels sing
   'Hallelujah' from ev'rything.
   Worshipping thee.

4. Cherubim – Seraphim – worship him
   Sun, moon and stars proclaim his power.
   Everyday – on our way – we shall say
   Hallelujah,

   'Hallelujah' the church bells ring,
   'Hallelujah' the angels sing
   'Hallelujah' from ev'rything.
   Hallelujah.

Silent Night

2. Silent night, holy night,
   Shepherds quake at the sight;
   Glories stream from heaven afar,
   Heav'nly hosts sing Alleluia!
   Christ the Saviour is born!
   Christ the Saviour is born!

3. Silent night, holy night,
   Son of God, love's pure light;
   Radiance beams from thy holy face,
   With the dawn of redeeming grace,
   Jesus, Lord at thy birth,
   Jesus, Lord at thy birth.

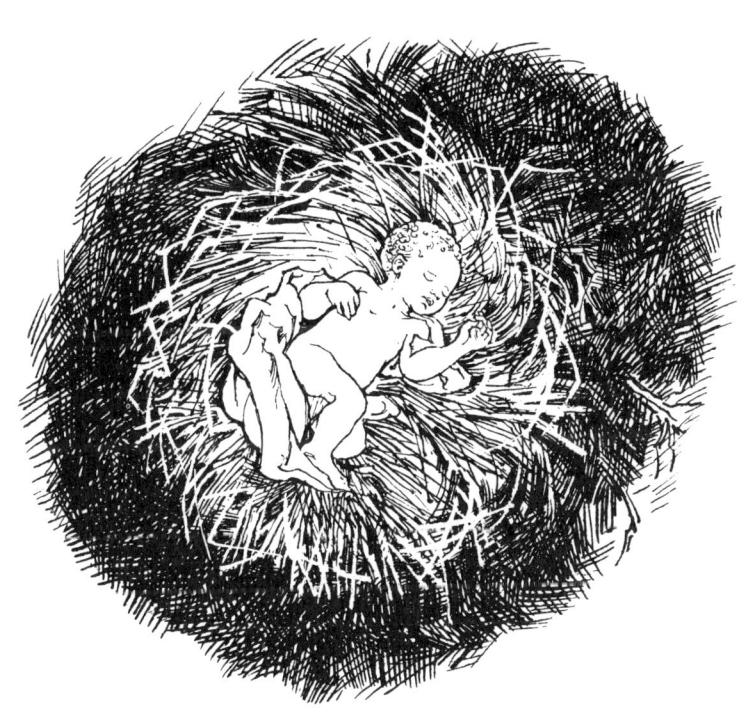

Good Christian Men Rejoice

*If we touch his tiny hand
Will he awake?*

And the first tree in the greenwood
It was the holly

For thy parting neither say nor sing by by

*Silent night, holy night
All is calm, all is bright*

I Saw Three Ships

2. And what was in those ships all three?
   On Christmas Day, on Christmas Day,
   And what was in those ships all three?
   On Christmas Day in the morning.

3. Our Saviour Christ and his lady.

4. Pray whither sailed those ships all three?

5. O they sailed into Bethlehem.

6. And all the bells on earth shall ring.

7. Then let us all rejoice again!

Il Est Né Le Divin Enfant

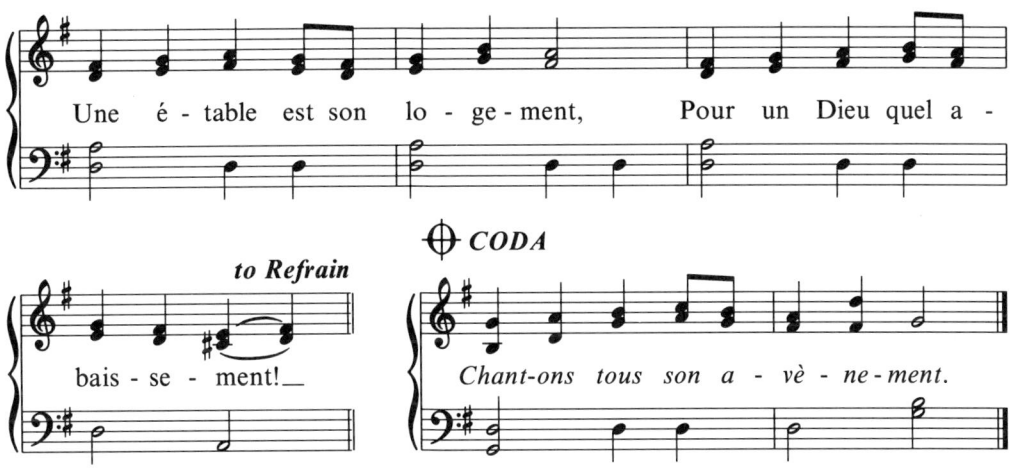

2. *Il est né le divin enfant,*
   Jouez hautbois, résonnez musettes,
   Il est né le divin enfant,
   Chantons tous son avènement.

   Ah! qu'il est beau, qu'il est charmant,
   Ah! que ses grâces sont parfaites!
   Qu'il est beau, qu'il est charmant,
   Qu'il est doux, ce divin enfant.

3. *Il est né etc.*

   O Jésus, roi tout puissant,
   Si petit enfant que vous êtes;
   O Jésus, roi tout puissant,
   Régnez sur nous entièrement.

Unto Us A Child Is Born

2   Cradled in a stall was he
      With sleepy cows and asses;
      But the very beasts could see
      That he all men surpasses.

3   Herod then with fear was filled:
      'A prince,' he said, 'in Jewry!'
      All the little boys he killed
      At Bethlehem in his fury.

4   Now may Mary's son, who came
      So long ago to love us,
      Lead us all with hearts aflame
      Unto the joys above.

5   Omega and Alpha he!
      Let the organ thunder,
      While the choir with peals of glee,
      Doth rend the air asunder.

God Rest You Merry Gentlemen

joy; O tidings of comfort and joy.

2. In Bethlehem in Jewry
   This blessed babe was born,
   And laid within a manger
   Upon this blessed morn;
   The which his mother Mary
   Did nothing take in scorn.

3. From God, our heavenly Father,
   A blessed angel came,
   And unto certain shepherds
   Brought tidings of the same,
   That there was born in Bethlehem
   The Son of God by name.

   O tidings of comfort and joy, comfort and joy!
   O tidings of comfort and joy!

4. But when they came to Bethlehem
   Where our dear Saviour lay,
   They found him in a manger,
   Where oxen feed on hay;
   His mother, Mary, kneeling,
   Unto the Lord did pray.

   O tidings of comfort and joy, etc.

5. Now to the Lord sing praises,
   All you within this place,
   And with true love and brotherhood
   Each other now embrace;
   This holy tide of Christmas
   All others doth deface.

   O tidings of comfort and joy, etc.

Sans Day Carol

2. Now the holly bears a berry as green as the grass,
   And Mary bore Jesus who died on the cross:

   *And Mary bore Jesus Christ our Saviour for to be
   And the first tree in the greenwood it was the holly,
   Holly, Holly! And the first tree in the greenwood it was the holly.*

3. Now the holly bears a berry as black as the coal,
   And Mary bore Jesus who died for us all:

   And Mary bore Jesus etc.

4. Now the holly bears a berry as blood it is red,
   Then Mary bore Jesus, who rose from the dead:

   And Mary bore Jesus etc.

The Holly and the Ivy

1. The hol-ly and the i-vy when they are both full grown, of__ all the trees that are in the wood the__ hol-ly bears the crown.

Refrain
O the ris-ing of the sun__ and the run-ning of the deer, the__ play-ing of the mer-ry or-gan, sweet sing-ing in the choir.

2. The holly bears a blossom,
   As white as the lily flower,
   And Mary bore sweet Jesus Christ,
   To be our sweet Saviour:

   O the rising of the sun
   And the running of the deer,
   The playing of the merry organ,
   Sweet singing in the choir.

3. The holly bears a berry,
   As red as any blood,
   And Mary bore sweet Jesus Christ,
   To do poor sinners good:

   O the rising of the sun etc.

4. The holly bears a prickle,
   As sharp as any thorn,
   And Mary bore sweet Jesus Christ,
   On Christmas Day in the morn:

   O the rising of the sun etc.

5. The holly bears a bark,
   As bitter as any gall,
   And Mary bore sweet Jesus Christ,
   For to redeem us all:

   O the rising of the sun etc.

In the Bleak Mid-Winter

2. Our God, heav'n cannot hold him
   Nor earth sustain;
   Heav'n and earth shall flee away
   When he comes to reign:
   In the bleak midwinter
   A stable place sufficed
   The Lord God almighty
   Jesus Christ.

3. Enough for him whom Cherubim
   Worship night and day
   A breastful of milk
   And a mangerful of hay;
   Enough for him, whom angels
   Fall down before,
   The ox and ass and camel
   Which adore.

4. Angels and Archangels
   May have gather'd there,
   Cherubim and Seraphim
   Throng'd the air,
   But only his mother
   In her maiden bliss
   Worshipped the beloved
   With a kiss.

5. What can I give him
   Poor as I am?
   If I were a shepherd
   I would bring a lamb;
   If I were a wise man
   I would do my part
   Yet what I can I give him
   Give my heart.

Masters in this Hall

2. Shepherds many on one
   Sat among the sheep,
   No man spake more word
   Than they had been sleep:

   Nowell! Nowell! etc.

3. Then to Bethlem town
   We went two and two,
   And in a sorry place
   Heard the oxen low:

   Nowell! Nowell! etc.

4. Therein did we see
   A sweet and goodly may
   And a fair old man,
   Upon the straw she lay:

   Nowell! Nowell! etc.

5. And a little child
   On her arm had she,
   'Wot ye who this is?'
   Said the hinds to me:

   Nowell! Nowell! etc.

6. This is Christ the Lord,
   Masters be ye glad!
   Christmas is come in,
   And no folk should be sad:

   Nowell! Nowell! etc.

Patapan

**Nowell, nowell
Born is the King of Israel**

See how the flow'rs all burst anew
Thinking snow is summer dew

And from steeple bid good people
Come adore the newborn King

*Fails my heart, I know not how;
I can go no longer*

Tomorrow Shall Be My Dancing Day

Up! Good Christen Folk and Listen

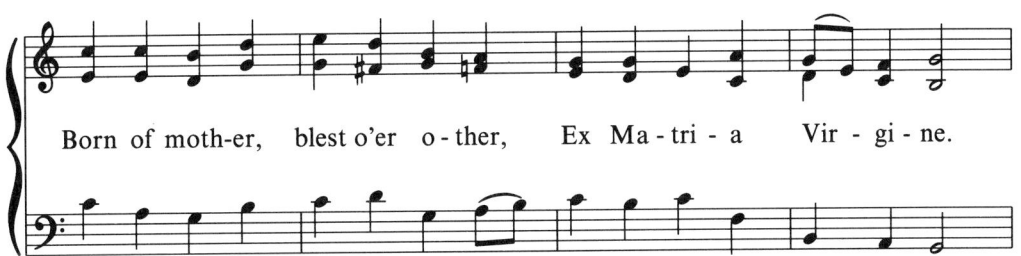

Born of moth-er, blest o'er o-ther, Ex Ma-tri a Vir-gi-ne.

In a sta-ble 'tis no fa-ble Chri-stus na-tus ho - di - e.

It is suggested that the first four bars are repeated at the end.

Good King Wenceslas

2. 'Hither, page, and stand by me,
   If thou know'st it, telling,
   Yonder peasant, who is he?
   Where and what his dwelling?'
   'Sire, he lives a good league hence,
   Underneath the mountain,
   Right against the forest fence,
   By St Agnes' fountain.'

3. 'Bring me flesh and bring me wine.
   Bring me pine-logs hither:
   Thou and I will see him dine.
   When we bear them thither.'
   Page and monarch, forth they went,
   Forth they went together;
   Through the rude wind's wild lament
   And the bitter weather.

4. 'Sire, the night is darker now.
   And the wind blows stronger;
   Fails my heart, I know not how;
   I can go no longer.'
   'Mark my footsteps, good my page;
   Tread thou in them boldly:
   Thou shalt find the winter's rage
   Freeze thy blood less coldly.'

5. In his master's steps he trod,
   Where the snow lay dinted;
   Heat was in the very sod
   Which the saint had printed.
   Therefore, Christian men, be sure,
   Wealth or rank possessing,
   Ye who now will bless the poor,
   Shall yourselves find blessing.

Shepherds! Shake off Your Drowsy Sleep

2. Hark! Even now, the bells ring round,
   Listen to their merry sound;
   Hark! How the birds new songs are making
   As if winter's chains were breaking!

   Shepherds! The chorus come and swell!
   Sing Noel, oh sing Noel!

3. See how the flow'rs all burst anew,
   Thinking snow is summer dew;
   See how the stars afresh are glowing,
   All their brightest beams bestowing.

   Shepherds! The chorus etc.

4. Cometh at length the age of peace
   Strife and sorrow now shall cease;
   Prophets foretold the wondrous story
   Of this heav'n-born Prince of Glory.

   Shepherds! The chorus etc.

5. Shepherds! Then up and quick away,
   Seek the Babe 'ere break of day;
   He is the hope of ev'ry nation
   All in Him shall find salvation.

   Shepherds! The chorus etc.

The First Nowell

2. They looked up and saw a star,
   Shining in the east, beyond them far,
   And to the earth it gave great light,
   And so it continued both day and night.

   Nowell, Nowell, Nowell, Nowell,
   Born is the King of Israel.

3. And by the light of that same star,
   Three wisemen came from country far;
   To seek for a King was their intent,
   And to follow the star wherever it went.

   Nowell etc.

4. This star drew nigh unto the north-west,
   O'er Bethlehem it took its rest,
   And there it did both stop and stay,
   Right over the place where Jesus lay.

   Nowell etc.

5. Then entered in those wisemen three,
   Full reverently upon their knee,
   And offered there, in his presence,
   Their gold, and myrrh, and frankincense.

   Nowell etc.

6. Then let us all with one accord,
   Sing praises to our heavenly Lord,
   That hath made heaven and earth of nought,
   And with his blood mankind hath bought.

   Nowell etc.

We Wish You a Merry Christmas

2. We all want some figgy pudding,
   We all want some figgy pudding,
   We all want some figgy pudding,
   So bring some right here!

   Good tidings we bring
   Of Jesus your King
   We wish you a merry Christmas
   And a happy new year!

3. We won't go until we get some,
   We won't go until we get some,
   We won't go until we get some,
   So bring some right here!

   Good tidings we bring etc.

Here We Come A-Wassailing

2. Our wassail cup is made
   Of the rosemary tree,
   And so is your beer
   Of the best barley.

   Love and joy come to you,
   And to you your wassail too,
   And God bless you, and send you
   A Happy New Year,
   And God send you a happy New Year

3. We are not daily beggars
   That beg from door to door,
   But we are neighbours' children
   Whom you have seen before.

   Love and joy etc.

4. Bring us out a table,
   And spread it with a cloth;
   Bring us out a mouldy cheese,
   And some of your Christmas loaf.

   Love and joy etc.

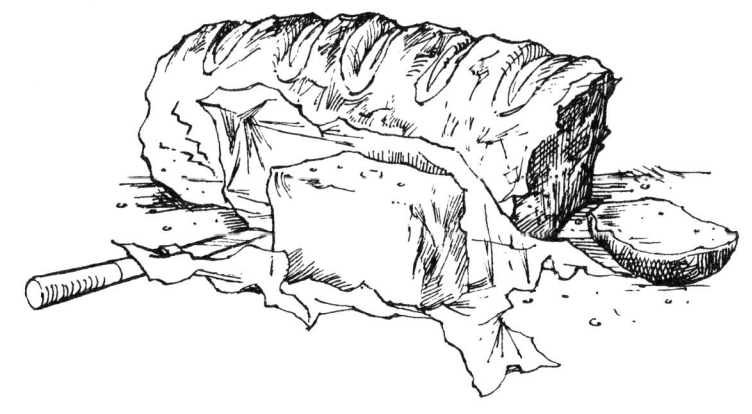

We Three Kings

2. Born a King on Bethlehem's plain,
   Gold I bring, to crown him again,
   King for ever, ceasing never,
   Over us all to reign.

   O star of wonder
   Star of night,
   Star with royal beauty bright,
   Westward leading still proceeding,
   Guide us to thy perfect light.

3. Frankincense to offer have I,
   Incense owns a Deity nigh.
   Prayer and praising, all men raising
   Worship him, God most high.

   O star of wonder etc.

4. Myrrh is mine, its bitter perfume
   Breathes a life of gathering gloom;
   Sorrowing, sighing, bleeding, dying,
   Sealed in the stone-cold tomb.

   O star of wonder etc.

5. Glorious now behold him arise,
   King and God and sacrifice,
   Alleluia, Alleluia;
   Earth to the heavens replies.

   O star of wonder etc.

O'er the Hill and o'er the Vale

Now through Syrian lands they go

Gold I bring . . . Frankincense to offer have I . . . Myrrh is mine

'Oh you,' he cooed, 'so good and true,
My beauty do I give to you—'

Eleven ladies dancing . . .

Easter Eggs

Coventry Carol

2. Herod, the king, in his raging, chargèd he hath this day,
   His men of might, in his own sight, all young children to slay.

   Lully, lulla, you little tiny child,
   By, by, lully, lullay.

3. That woe is me, poor child for thee! And ever morn and day,
   For thy parting neither say nor sing by by, lully lullay!

   Lully, lulla, etc.

The Twelve Days of Christmas

1. A partridge in a pear tree
2. Two turtle doves
3. Three french hens
4. Four colly birds
5. Five gold rings
6. Six geese a-laying
7. Seven swans a-swimming
8. Eight maids a-milking
9. Nine drummers drumming
10. Ten pipers piping
11. Eleven ladies dancing
12. Twelve lords a-leaping

The Infant King

1. Sing lul-la-by! Lul-la-by ba-by, now re-clin-ing. Sing lul-la-by! Hush, do not wake the in-fant King. An-gels are watch-ing, stars are shin-ing o-ver the place where he is ly-ing. Sing lul-la-by.

2. Sing lullaby!
   Lullaby baby, now a-sleeping,
   Sing lullaby!
   Hush, do not wake the infant King,
   Soon will come sorrow with the morning,
   Soon will come bitter grief and weeping:
   Sing lullaby!

3. Sing lullaby!
   Lullaby baby, now a-dozing,
   Sing lullaby!
   Hush, do not wake the infant King,
   Soon comes the cross, the nails, the piercing,
   Then in the grave at last reposing
   Sing lullaby!

4. Sing lullaby!
   Lullaby! Is the babe a-waking?
   Sing lullaby!
   Hush, do not stir the infant King.
   Dreaming of Easter, gladsome morning,
   Conquering Death, its bondage breaking:
   Sing lullaby!

The Birds

2. A pigeon flew over to Galilee,
   Vrercroo.
   He strutted and cooed, and was full of glee,
   Vrercroo.
   And showed with jewelled wings unfurled,
   His joy that Christ was in the world,
   Vrercroo, vrercroo, vrercroo.

3. A dove settled down upon Nazareth,
   Tsucroo.
   And tenderly chanted with all his breath
   Tsucroo:
   'O you,' he cooed, 'so good and true,
   My beauty do I give to you–'
   Tsucroo, tsucroo, tsucroo.

This Joyful Eastertide

2. My flesh in hope shall rest,
   And for a season slumber:
   Till trump from east to west
   Shall wake the dead in number:

   Had Christ, that once was slain,
   Ne'er burst his three-day prison,
   Our faith had been in vain:
   But now hath Christ arisen.

3. Death's flood hath lost his chill,
   Since Jesus crossed the river:
   Lover of souls, from ill
   My passing soul deliver:

   Had Christ, etc.

Index of First Lines

Away in a manger	14
Easter Eggs! Easter Eggs!	65
From out of a wood did a cuckoo fly, cuckoo	72
Girls and boys, leave your toys, make no noise	28
God rest you merry gentlemen	38
Good Christian men rejoice	32
Good King Wenceslas looked out	52
Hark! The herald angels sing	24
Here we come a-wassailing	60
How far is it to Bethlehem?	26
Il est né le divin enfant	34
In the bleak mid-winter	44
Infant Holy	16
I saw three ships come sailing in	33
Little Jesus, sweetly sleep, do not stir	17
Lully, lulla, you little tiny child	66
Masters in this hall	46
Now the holly bears a berry as white as the milk	40
O come all ye faithful	22
O'er the hill and o'er the vale	64
O little town of Bethlehem	20
Once in royal David's city	18
On the first day of Christmas my true love sent to me	68
Shepherds! Shake off your drowsy sleep.	54
Silent night, holy night	30
Sing lullaby	70
The angel Gabriel from heaven came	12
The first Nowell the angel did say	56
The holly and the ivy	42
This joyful Eastertide	74
Tomorrow shall be my dancing day	49
Unto us a child is born	36
Up! Good Christen folk and listen	50
We three kings of Orient are	62
We wish you a merry Christmas	58
Willie take your little drum,	48